D0855073

Full Throttle

Ford GT

Tracy Nelson Maurer

Rourke
Publishing LLC
Vero Beach, Florida 32964

www.rourkepublishing.com

PHOTO CREDITS: All photos courtesy of Ford Motor Company

Project Assistance: William "Lynn" Larsen and www.GT40.com

Also, the author extends appreciation to Julie Lundgren, Forest Lake Ford, Mike Maurer, Lois M. Nelson, and the team at Rourke Publishing.

Editor: Robert Stengard-Olliges
Page Design: Tara Raymo

Notice: The publisher recognizes that some words, model names, and designations mentioned herein are the property of the trademark holder. They are used for identification purposes only. This is not an official publication.

Library of Congress Cataloging-in-Publication Data

Maurer, Tracy, 1965-
  Ford GT / Tracy Nelson Maurer.
      p. cm. -- (Full throttle 2)
  Includes bibliographical references and index.
  ISBN 978-1-60044-571-2
  1. Ford GT40 automobile--Juvenile literature. I. Title.
  TL215.F7M327 2008
  629.222'1--dc22
                                    2007014442

Printed in the USA

IG/IG

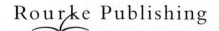

Rourke Publishing

www.rourkepublishing.com – rourke@rourkepublishing.com
Post Office Box 3328, Vero Beach, FL 32964

Table of Contents

Built to Win

The French city of Le Mans (say: la MAH) welcomes thousands of racing fans every June. Since 1923, the 24 Hours of Le Mans **endurance** race has tested the world's top **marques** and their drivers on its 8.4-mile (13.5-km) course. Winners enjoy a lifetime of bragging rights. Back in 1962, Henry Ford II wanted to claim a victory at Le Mans. First he tried to buy Enzo Ferrari's company, which had won many times there. No go. So Ford decided he would build a Ford Motor Company car to beat the Italians.

Le Mans drivers cover about 3,100 miles (5,000 km) in 24 hours.

Ford engineers worked in Great Britain with Europe's top racecar frame designers. They built an entirely new racecar with only one purpose: Win at Le Mans.

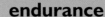

endurance
> the power or strength to keep going a long distance or long time

marque
> the logo for an automobile manufacturer or its models

prototype
> for carmakers, the first working model of a design

Fast Fact

Ford unveiled the first Ford GT **prototype** at the 1964 New York International Auto Show.

Former racecar driver Carroll Shelby powered up the early Ford GT40 Mark I car with a 7.0-liter V-8 motor to create the Ford GT40 Mark II. And, yes, that's the same Carroll Shelby who created the Shelby Cobra and beefed up the Ford Mustang and the Dodge Viper.

Ford started to collect checkered flags in 1966. The **mid-engine** Ford GT40 Mark II won at the International Challenge Cup for Sports Prototypes, Daytona 24-hour Continental, and Sebring 12-hour Endurance Race. Then 400,000 fans at the 1966 24 Hours of Le Mans watched in awe as the Ford GT40 totally dusted the competition. Ford swept the top three spots.

In 1966, the Ford GT40 set a new Le Mans record when it topped 200 mph (322 km/h) on the Mulsanne Straight.

Ford named the car "GT" to show its racing goal: *gran turismo* (grand touring) race courses. Why the number 40? The car stood only 40 inches (102 cm) tall.

The Ford GT40s were so far ahead of other cars at the 1966
Le Mans that the drivers had time to set up a "tie" at the finish.
The judges gave the win to the car that had started farther
back, since it had covered more distance in the 24 hours.

Ten Ford GT40s raced at Le Mans in 1967,
including the Mark I, Mark II, and the new
Mark IV. The Mark IV used the Mark II engine
but a lighter aluminum honeycomb **chassis**
instead of heavy steel. Again, the Ford GT won.

The Ford GT40 did not display
a number 40 on its outside
panels or inside emblems.

The same Ford GT40 won the same race twice (Le Mans in 1968 and 1969), a new record.

Milestones at Le Mans

- **1966** Le Mans: Ford GT Mark II cars finished in 1st Place, 2nd Place, and 3rd Place
- **1967** Le Mans: Ford GT Mark IV cars finished in 1st Place and 4th Place
- **1968** Le Mans: Ford GT40 Mark I finished in 1st Place
- **1969** Le Mans: Ford GT40 Mark I cars finished in 1st Place and 3rd Place

Ford quit building GT40s in 1966, rolling out fewer than 200 of the cars. But the GT40's record-breaking streak at Le Mans made it an instant motoring legend. Ford used its experience building the GT40 to improve other company vehicles, especially the Mustang. The Ford GT40 also inspired other marques' supercars, such as the Lamborghini Miura and Dodge Viper.

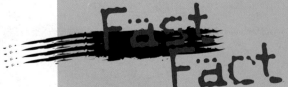

The Ford GT won the 1969 Le Mans by only two seconds—a breathless finish for a race that lasts 24 hours.

Old Made New

Ford Motor Company celebrated its 100th anniversary in 2003 by creating a new Ford GT supercar that stirred memories of the 1960s Le Mans winners. Ford wanted the design to look like the original two-seater. It had to fly with blinding speed and hug hairpin corners. But Ford meant for this car to rule the streets, not the racetracks.

Fast Fact

Ford called the new GT "the pace car for an entire company."

Many Ford fans liked how the round headlights in the new Ford GT looked like the number "100" in honor of the company's centennial.

concept car
a vehicle built to try out new looks and techniques

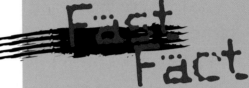

Fast Off The Drawing Board

Ford engineers used advanced computer testing to cut two years off the time it usually takes to move a car from the drawing board to production.

- **2002** - The new Ford GT **concept car** first dazzled fans at the North American Auto Show.
- **2003** - Prototypes rolled out in time for Ford's centennial parade.
- **2004** - Production started and Ford delivered the first Ford GTs to customers by September.

Ford dropped the number 40 from the name of the new GT. That's the fastest way to tell the two versions apart.

Television commercials before the 2004 Super Bowl game gave millions of viewers a peek at the old-but-new Ford GT.

Look-Alike Cars

Ford designers created the Ford GT from the outside in. They echoed the original GT40's flowing lines and sleek, cat-like stance. Just as important, they cleverly blended modern equipment into the classic design to make the new car safe, comfortable, and **street-legal**. Many people confuse the new two-seater Ford GT for the 1960s version.

To protest the dangers of running across the track to start the Le Mans race, driver Jacky Ickx slowly walked to his GT40 in 1969. He dodged a few cars (or they dodged him) as they blasted onto the course. Jacky pulled his car onto the track last. His team still won the race.

J Mays, who worked on the wildly successful new Volkswagen Beetle in the 1990s, also helped with the new Ford GT.

Like the original, the Ford GT does not have door handles. Instead, a small rubber push-button under the window ledge opens the door.

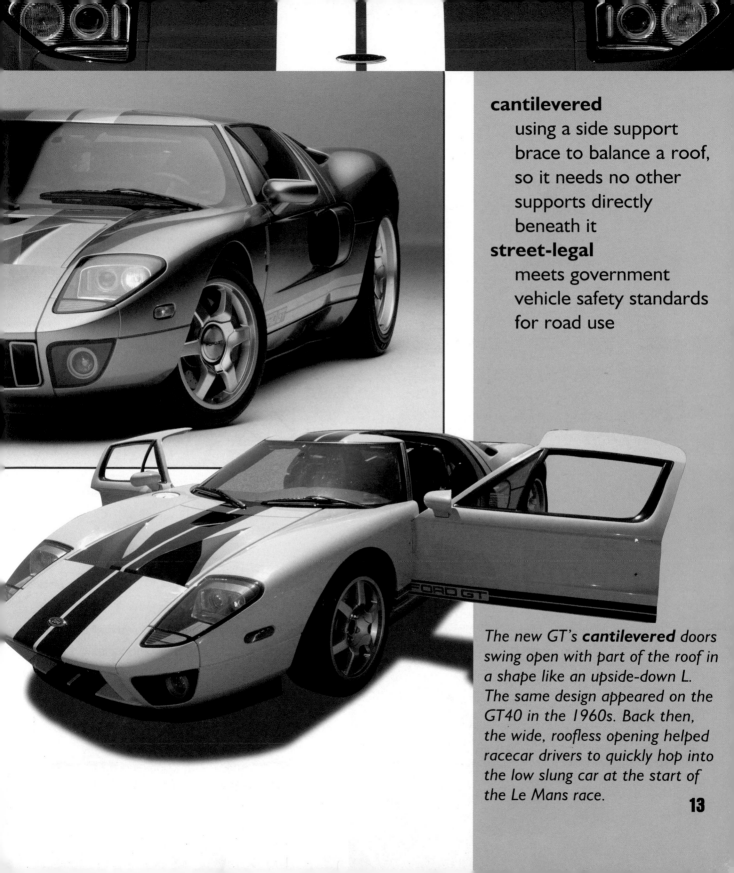

cantilevered
using a side support brace to balance a roof, so it needs no other supports directly beneath it

street-legal
meets government vehicle safety standards for road use

*The new GT's **cantilevered** doors swing open with part of the roof in a shape like an upside-down L. The same design appeared on the GT40 in the 1960s. Back then, the wide, roofless opening helped racecar drivers to quickly hop into the low slung car at the start of the Le Mans race.*

13

Fast Fact

The wraparound windshield looks similar on both the classic and modern models.

Engineers wedged a small "trunk" under the car's hood in both the 1960s and modern versions. A backpack could fit in it, but not much more.

aerodynamic
> shaped for air to flow
> easily over the body at
> higher speeds

*Like the Ford GT40, the
Ford GT looks ready to pounce with its
huge haunches curved over the back wheels. The
rear end still sweeps into the classic ducktail spoiler,
too. This helps improve the **aerodynamics** that
keep the car from lifting off the road at high speeds.*

The Ford GT measures
longer and wider than the
original. It also stands taller
at 44.3 inches (112 cm).

Customers receive a vinyl
number kit for a personalized
racecar look.

The Racy Ride Inside

Racecars need hardworking and lightweight equipment, not cushy cockpits. The 1960s Ford GT40s kept a sparse interior. The new Ford GT borrows design cues from the old racing days. It also surrounds the driver in comfort.

Toggle switches control the headlamps, fog lights, rear defrost, and windshield wipers. The 1960s GT40s had similar switches.

Unlike the old GT40, the new car's shift lever angles toward the driver for more comfy shifting.

tachometer
an instrument for measuring speed of rotation in revolutions per minute (rpms)

Both the old and new Ford supercars use a speedometer with a dial and needle, not digital displays. It's set off to the far right. The **tachometer**, also with a dial and needle, anchors the center position in front of the driver.

The Ford GT set a new standard by showing rare magnesium on the center floor console and radio bracket. Other cars had used this sturdy but lightweight metal before, but not where anyone could see its sleek gray finish. The GT also uses it instead of heavier aluminum for seat frames, support brackets, and instrument panels.

Like all decent supercars, the Ford GT roars to life with a push-button starter. Turn the key, press in the clutch, and press "start." Then hang on!

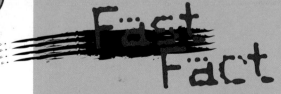

The GT40 cleared the windshield with a single wiper. The new GT has two wipers.

17

Cool Comfort

Air-conditioning helps the Ford GT cabin feel more comfortable than the original that skipped this weighty option. Back then, a driver could cool off zipping around the track. But drivers in the city on a summer day usually felt steam-baked in minutes with the hot engine just inches behind the seat.

Style stretches from head to toe in the Ford GT. Race-inspired lightweight aluminum pedals control the accelerator, clutch, and brakes.

Fast Fact

Tall people felt pinched in the 1960s cockpit. The new version offers more room.

The 1960s drivers listened to a very loud motor and that's about it. Not today's Ford GT rockers. They're tuned into a stereo that can blast louder than the eight-cylinder powerhouse—but who really wants to block out that beastly purr?

Holes in those fine leather seats serve a real purpose. The ventilated pattern helps cool the driver and passenger. The seat shape also keeps them snugly in place on fast corners.

The Marvel's Secrets

The new Ford GT mirrors the original's looks and its trophy snatching attitude. In addition to the fine retro styling, this supercar is a modern engineering marvel like the first one was in its day. Peek under the shiny paint and bold racing stripes, and the chassis hints at the car's secrets to asphalt shredding performance.

The chassis tunnel protects the cigar-shaped "ship-in-a-bottle" fuel tank. The entire fuel system tucks inside the tank, including the fuel pumps, sensors, and filters. The fuel tank holds 17.5 gallons (66.24 liters) of 91-octane gasoline.

Fast Fact

The GT cruises about 280 miles (450 km) on one tank. At 200 mph (322 km/h), that's a fill-up every hour and twenty minutes or so.

Good Reasons To Use A "Ship-in-a-Bottle" Fuel Tank

- Saves space
- Keeps gasoline from sloshing at fast starts
- Helps lock in gas vapors
- Balances the car
- Allows a low stance

The extrusion process forces hot aluminum through a form, like squeezing Play-Doh through a Fun Factory.

extruded aluminum formed by forcing hot aluminum through a specially shaped opening to make a strong, lightweight part

*A clever lightweight aluminum tunnel runs down the center of the chassis like a rigid backbone. For extra strength, 35 **extruded aluminum** parts form the whole chassis.*

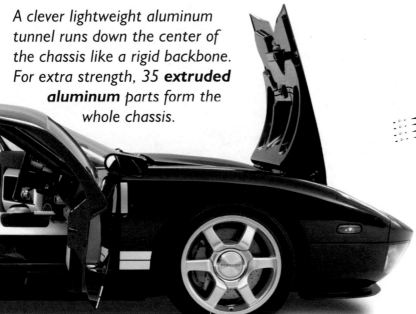

Fäst Fäct

The GT fuel-filler opening is on the front fender like the original GT40.

The hinged cover pops open with a pull on the side handle. The pump nozzle slips right into the capless filler tube. A racecar styled gas seal makes this a cool first for a road car.

Engineers used computers to tweak the car's aerodynamic design. A modern construction process allowed the new aluminum body panels to follow complex shapes. No more muscle wrenching labor to make front hood scoops or to fit door panels into place. Now one single aluminum piece forms each door to the exact curves and size of the design, over and over again.

A lower "chin" spoiler splits airflow to help keep the nose from lifting at high speeds. The smooth front end seems to lack a bumper, similar to the original car. That's not street-legal today. The design neatly hides a safety bumper within the nose frame.

Fast Fact

Ford says it could build the car's structure with an accuracy near 1/10,000 inch (1/400 mm). A sheet of paper is about 40 times thicker than that.

Blast From The Past

In the 1770s, physics professor Giovanni Battista Venturi defined many rules that still apply to aerodynamics. He worked at Italy's University of Modena. Today, Modena is also home to Lamborghini, Ferrari, Maserati, and other supercar companies.

louvers
a series of narrow openings or slits that allow air in

Air scoops behind the doors and rear **louvers** over the engine breathe cool, fresh air into the engine. The air also feeds the engine's hungry supercharger to make more power.

Air flows smoothly under the car thanks to Venturi tunnels. The tunnels help direct air and shoot it out faster. This creates more downforce for better handling at high speeds.

23

The Ford GT's mid-mounted aluminum V-8 motor kicks out 550 horsepower. The GT40 could also hit that mark, but it needed a hefty 7.0-liter engine. It didn't have a supercharger like the new, smaller 5.4-liter motor does. The Ford GT's supercharger sucks in air, squeezes it and shoots it into the engine. The added air creates a bigger explosion in the cylinders for more power.

The rear window looks similar to the original. The window showcases the engine in action. It only opens from the inside.

The GT doesn't need to shift gears before it hits 60 mph (97 km/h). That helps it to accelerate like a rocket.

A fast car must stop quickly, too. The Ford GT uses big brakes on its big wheels and tires. Holes on the brakes keep the brakes clean and let heat escape.

Ford GT Engineering team certified a 205-mph (330-km/h) top speed during company tests. Other respected sources have clocked even higher speeds.

Several car magazines sent giddy reporters to test the Ford GT. They wrote about zooming from 0 to 60 mph (97 km/h) in 3.8 seconds.

Fast Fact

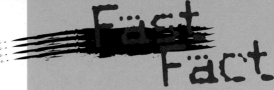

The Ford GT quickly halts from 60 mph (97 km/h) to 0 in just 109 feet (33 meters).

25

Racing Dreams

No matter how much the Ford GT looks like the famous GT40 racecar, Ford built it for the street—not the track. Many people still dream of racing the new Ford GT. Few have the money, resources, and skills to turn dreams into reality. Rebuilding a car, even one so close to its racing roots, costs hundreds of thousands of dollars to make it safe and fast. It must meet the racecourse rules, too.

The winning drivers at Doran Racing couldn't resist putting a new Ford GT on the track. Skilled engineers trimmed weight off the street model and boosted its aerodynamics. The team calls its prototype the Ford GT-R.

Popular Japanese driver Hidetoshi Mitsusada drove a Ford GT in the GT300 class of his country's Super GT race series. He hasn't won. Yet.

vintage
old, original, or classic

Ford GT40s still race in **vintage** car races, especially in America and Europe. The Le Mans Classic, a race only for historic cars, featured a special trophy in 2006 to honor the 40th anniversary of the Ford GT40 win.

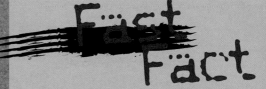

Fast Fact

After four decades, vintage GT40s still clock over 200 mph (322 km/h).

Ford stopped GT production in September 2006, forty years after the Le Mans victory. Just over 4,000 GTs were built. Collectors expect the car's value to increase in the future. They look for low production numbers, limited paint colors, and original parts on their purchases. A 2005 Ford GT in Quicksilver paint (only offered that year) sold for $530,000 in 2006. Its production number, 00003, was the lowest available to the public.

Fast Fact

Original Ford GT40s are worth $800,000 to $4 million, depending on each car's history.

A Ford GT costs well over $145,000. That's too pricey for many Ford GT fans. They can still take a virtual ride with video and computer games.

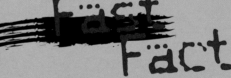

Fast Fact

Gran Turismo game developer Kazunori Yamauchi actually owned a Ford GT.

The Ford GT won new fans instead of checkered flags. Along the way, it revived the spirit of the first Ford supercar and earned bragging rights of its own.

Glossary

aerodynamic (ahr oh dih NAM ik) – shaped for air to flow easily over the body at higher speeds

cantilevered (KAN tuh lee vurd) – using a side support brace to balance a roof, so it needs no other supports directly beneath it

chassis (CHASS ee) – the frame that supports the body of a vehicle

concept car (KON sept KAR) – a vehicle built to try out new looks and techniques

endurance (en DOO rens) – the power or strength to keep going a long distance or long time

extruded aluminum (eks TROO ded uh LOO mi num) – formed by forcing hot aluminum through a specially shaped opening to make a strong, lightweight part

louvers (LOO vurz) – a series of narrow openings or slits that allow air in

marque (MARK) – the logo for an automobile manufacturer or its models

mid-engine (MID EN jin) – engine placement behind the passenger cabin but ahead of the rear axle; this balances the weight for better handling

prototype (PROH tah tihp) – for carmakers, the first working model of a design

street-legal (STREET LEE guhl) – meets government vehicle safety standards for road use

tachometer (tak AHM eh tur) – an instrument for measuring speed of rotation in revolutions per minute (rpms)

vintage (VIN tej) – old, original, or classic

Further Reading

Ford GT40: The Story from 1963 to the New GT Supercar. DVD, Duke Marketing Limit, 2006.

Padgett, Martin. *Hot Cars, Cool Rides*. Scholastic, 2005.

Streather, Adrian. *Ford GT: Then, and Now*. Veloce, 2006.

Wood, Jonathan. *The Ultimate History of Fast Cars*. Parragon Publishing, 2005.

Websites

www.fordvehicles.com/fordgt/

www.fordgttv.com

www.gt40s.com

www.gt40.org.uk

www.yououghttoknowthis.com

Index

About the Author

Tracy Nelson Maurer writes nonfiction and fiction books for children, including more than 60 titles for Rourke Publishing LLC. Tracy lives with her husband Mike and two children near Minneapolis, Minnesota.